Newbie's Guide to Meditation

A Simplified, Stripped Down, Bare Bones Guide on How to Meditate

By Lauren Darges and Larry Langbehn

Cover layout by Jules Schaafsma

Photo of Lauren by Michelle Feileacan Photography

Copyright © 2017 Lauren Darges and Larry Langbehn

All rights reserved.

ISBN: 978-1523774623

DEDICATION

This book is dedicated to all the newbie meditators
and to our teachers and guides who have
taught us to meditate.

CONTENTS

Acknowledgments   i

Nuts and Bolts 1
   Sitting 2
   Focusing 2
   Can't Hold Your Focus - It's Normal 3
   Get Going 4
   Do It Daily 5
   There is No Wrong Way 5

Refining Your Tools 7
   Meditation is Like a Tool 7
   Sitting Position is Important 7
   Tricks for Staying Focused 8
   Breath Counting 10
   Mental Noting or "Naming" 10
   Meditating with a Group 11

Itches, Twitchs and Other Bodily Distractions 12
   Itches 12
   The Sit Down Parts, Neck and Back 13
   Coughing and Sneezing 13
   Sleepiness 14
   Restlessness 14

Meditation Variations 17
   Mindfulness 18
   Mindful Awareness in Meditation 18
   Mindful Exploration 19
   Walking Meditation 20
   Body Scan Meditation 21
   Heart Coherence Meditation 22

Loving Kindness Meditation 23
Contemplative Meditation 24
Self Inquiry 25

Why Meditate? 26
What's Your Motivation? 27
How to Keep Your Practice Going 28

Recommended Reading 30

ACKNOWLEDGMENTS

Special thanks goes to Larry who birthed this book by pushing a document over to Lauren saying, "Here's what I think you should write about. People need this. I started it. What do you think?" Also a big thanks to Katherine Chargin for her thoughtful editing support, Christopher Kerr for design support and to Lauren's mastermind partner, Ben Brown, M.D., who encouraged her to "just do it."

CHAPTER 1

NUTS AND BOLTS

There is no magic or woo-woo stuff here. Meditation is, simply, a mental state characterized by having a calm mind while the mind also remains fully conscious and alert.

A calm mind just means quieting down all the chatter that our minds are typically doing. Achieving this state is fairly simple but does require a bit of work and some practice. It also requires some patience with yourself. It's a skill and, like all skills, it needs some effort and persistence to learn.

- Meditation requires some mental effort
- Meditation requires practice
- Learning meditation requires patience with oneself

The process is quite simple:

Sitting

Find a place to sit that is comfortable but not too comfortable. A straight-backed chair or using a pillow behind a sloped back chair is fine. Too comfortable and you go to sleep. Too ridged and it is distracting.

Close your eyes, settle into your chair, and spend a few moments relaxing yourself.

Now comes the first really important part:

Focusing

Use your mind to focus on one thing or event. For this level of learning, focus on your breath. Focus on how it feels coming in and going out and every sensation about the breath along the way. Focus on the physical sensation of the breath.

Where do you notice it most? Is it in your nostrils, your throat, your chest or belly? Wherever you notice it, that will be your point of focus which you keep coming back to. For example, watch your breath and feel it as your belly rises and falls with each inhale and exhale.

It requires an active mental effort to stay attentive to the breath. It may not be easy at first—it takes some practice and may seem odd at first.

The object of staying focused on the breath is to prevent the mind from being busy with other thoughts. If you are strongly focused on your breathing, there is no mental space left for "busy mind" to intrude.

Staying focused is the part that takes some effort of will. With time and practice, the mind begins to calm down and there are fewer interruptions from other thoughts. This is what our minds do under these conditions. Pretty soon you get to the calm mind and attentive state that is meditation.

Often when people first begin they tense or manipulate their breath in some way or become overly conscious of it. You might notice that you do this too by making your breath bigger than normal or longer than normal. There is no need to change the breath, no fancy yoga breathing needed. Just let your breath be. Feel it just as it is and watch it.

Now comes the second really important part:

Can't Hold Your Focus - It's Normal

You will find out very quickly that the busyness of all your thoughts *do* intrude on the focused breathing you are doing. You will find yourself making shopping lists or fantasizing about a sports event or going to a movie. The list of what we think about is endless. Our minds will, naturally, wander. This is just the way they work. However, every time you become aware that you are "out in the woods again," just go back to focusing on your breathing.

This is the part about having patience with your self. Understand clearly that a wandering mind is normal and try not to get flustered by it. Just bring your focus back to your breath and do it without any self-criticism. No phooeys or darns or any stuff like that are allowed.

Get Going

Frequently, someone's first experience with meditation is in a group setting with other people that are practiced meditators. A typical sitting time is anywhere from 25 to 40 minutes. As a "first timer," you may not be able to focus for the full time of the sitting. What to do? Well, the best thing to do is to let go of trying and just sit there quietly and relax with your thoughts for the rest of the sitting period. If that doesn't work for you, then as quietly as possible, get up and leave.

Everyone has a different learning capability. Some people can pick this up within a few tries and others require longer. Do what you can and if it's only a few minutes, that's OK. Use the timer on your i-thingy to help you keep track. Increase the sitting time as your skill allows.

> IMPORTANT: This is enough information to get you going. You will rapidly pick up a great deal of information just by meditating and from being around others that have an existing practice.

Here is the third really important thing:

Do It Daily

Do this regularly! Do it every day even if only for a few minutes. This is how building the skill of meditation is accomplished.

The more you do it, the longer and more easily you will be able to do it. The initial objective is to get to the point that you are comfortable meditating for 15 to 20 minutes. Once you achieve this skill level, you will be able to jump to 40 minutes in a group setting.

Now, the fourth really important thing:

There is No Wrong Way

There is no wrong way to do this!!! Get IT! *There is no wrong way to do this.* You are meditating for yourself and nobody else. Find your own level of comfort with meditation.

Two of the immediate benefits of meditation are that it is very, very relaxing and you can carry this relaxation forward into your daily life. Also, if you have trouble getting back to sleep after waking up at night, using the focused breathing is a great way to relax your mind and allow sleep to come.

CHAPTER 2

REFINING YOUR TOOLS

Meditation is Like a Tool

At level 2, you are still learning certain skills about how to use your meditation tool. At level 4, you will get a smattering of information on how this clear and alert mind state can be applied. Patience, please.

Sitting Position is Important

Sitting posture is very important. This becomes clear as your sitting time increases. If you can sit on the floor, that's great but, as Westerners, we usually sit in chairs and have lost that floor-sitting-flexibility. No problem. Just find a suitable chair.

You need to find a sitting position that is comfortable

nough that you can sit for 40 minutes without great discomfort and not so comfortable that you fall asleep. The easiest way to do this is to sit upright in a comfortable chair with a vertical spine. It helps if the seat of the chair is somewhat firm.

Leaning against the back of a chair or a slope-backed chair is often too comfortable. A sloped back chair also gives you a sloped-back spine rather than a vertical spine. If a slope backed chair is all that is available, use a pillow to hold yourself vertical or sit forward in the chair without back support.

For many people, sitting forward on the chair with a pillow under the hips provides the perfect posture. When the hips are a little higher than the knees, the spine is naturally straight and relaxed.

You will need to do a little experimentation to find what is best for you. You are aiming for a straight spine and an alert, but relaxed posture.

Tricks for Staying Focused

Pretty much always, we need help to stay focused on our breathing and keep our random thoughts from intruding. There are simple mental tricks to help us do this. They have the common feature of occupying more mental space than simply focusing on the breath. Most frequently it's a pair of words or sayings that are stated along with breathing in and breathing out.

The following examples are words that are an observation of what you are doing:

    Inhale: I am breathing in.

    Exhale: I am breathing out.

This is fairly long and can be shortened:

    Inhale: Breathing in

    Exhale: Breathing out

Or simply:

    Inhale: In

    Exhale: Out

A variation of this is the following:

"Breathing in, I calm my body and mind."

"Breathing out, I calm my fear" (or anxiety, or any negative emotion).

The following example is instructional. It tells us to do something:

    Inhale: Let

    Exhale: Go

"Let/Go" is a really good way of initially relaxing. Each time you do a cycle with these words, focus on some body area and release it. It's a good way for starting meditation.

The following example is of words that are inherently so powerful that they command our attention:

    Inhale: Love   Exhale: God

                   Or

    Inhale: I   Exhale: Am

Breath Counting

Another technique is breath counting. Each exhale is one count. You watch and count each exhale, until you get to ten. Then you start back at one.

If you get distracted at any point and your mind wanders, simply start again at one. In meditation we have the opportunity to begin again, many, many times, when the mind wanders.

See what works best for you. Once you find the technique that works for you, stick with it over time. This will help you in gaining depth in your practice.

Mental Noting or "Naming"

Another trick is that when you notice that your mind has been wandering around the universe or you've been thinking about what to make for dinner and you catch it, you can name what you've been doing— "wandering," "reverie," "planning," "last night's movie,"—and simply return attention to your breath.

Remember, each time you notice your mind wandering is a small victory in your meditation practice. So, celebrate and be kind to yourself when you catch your wandering mind.

Meditating with a Group

Meditating regularly with a group is a key element to a successful mediation practice. There are a number of benefits, such as:

- Easier to meditate in a group

- Can help you stay inspired with your home practice

- Helpful to have a good instructor who can support you as your learn and grow

- Opportunity for spiritual community and friendship

CHAPTER 3

ITCHES, TWITCHS AND OTHER BODILY DISTRACTIONS

Well, surprise, we're human and many things can interrupt the mental focus used when meditating. This level is about the physical things.

Itches

This is the single most common source of physical distraction and, actually, the easiest to deal with. Instead of trying to ignore an itch until it goes away, do the opposite. Actively observe the itch while meditating. What's it feel like? How irritating is it? What about the area immediately surrounding the itch?

You get the idea. Most itches have no more than a 90 second lifetime, tops. By observing an itch, we diminish its impact.

The Sit Down Parts, Neck and Back

If you need to change posture to relieve a persistent discomfort, do so. But before automatically adjusting your body, stop and take note of the sensation. Is it hot, achy, numb, stabbing, clenching? How big is it? Does it have a color?

Sometimes simply exploring and being curious about the sensation or discomfort changes it. After exploring, if you choose to move, move slowly and with intention. Try not to move habitually.

Coughing and Sneezing

Many times when we cough, it's not really necessary. Other times, it most certainly is. Nobody in a sitting group expects you to be uncomfortable. It doesn't serve the purpose of meditating. As a courtesy to others, simply ask yourself, "Is this, really, necessary at this time?" What is the sensation of the cough? Notice it. Observe it. If you really need to, cough and be done with it.

If you feel a genuine coughing fit coming on, and you

are with others in a group, just quietly leave the room and return when it's over.

Sneezing works much the same way but does tend to be more insistent. So just get it over with and return to your focus.

Sleepiness

Every meditator struggles with sleepiness at some point. If you are sleepy, make sure you are sitting up straight. You can also open your eyes and gaze down at the floor.

When you find yourself drifting off, you can make a strong mental note about what is happening; "sleeping, sleeping, sleeping," or "drifting off" or "sleepy." Sometimes we have to state the observation strongly to ourselves a few times to help snap us out of it.

If the sleepiness continues and this technique doesn't break through, it's ok to end the meditation. It is also, however, a great feeling—and a clearing of the mind—to overcome the sleepiness by simply being patient and persistent. When you get to the other side, and sleepiness clears, the mind is refreshed.

Restlessness

Sometimes when we sit for meditation we are very restless and feel like we are about to jump out of our skin. This is another passing state. Yes, really, it will pass.

If you find yourself in this experience, try standing up, stretching your arms up toward the ceiling and taking three long, slow, deep breaths.

When you sit down, see if you can put your attention on where your body is contacting your chair or cushion (your hips, buttocks, back of your legs). Feel yourself, your body, fully sitting there. Notice the quality of your body on the chair. Is it heavy or light, soft or hard, warm or cool? See if you can feel your whole body sitting there from head to toe. Resume your meditation.

You can also apply a mindful focus to the sensation of restlessness. Can you notice where in your body the restlessness is coming from? Is there an originating point? Or is it a general overall agitated feeling in the body?

Name the sensation as best you can—jittery, snake-like, prickly, achy, whatever it is—and watch the sensation of the restlessness while being with your breath simultaneously.

When we say "watch the sensation" this means to feel it, if you can. Sense into the body sensation of restlessness while being with your breath. You can do this for any body sensation that comes up: achy back, knees, stomach ache. This can often transform the physical sensation.

Even if it is difficult and it seems like you are having no success, please be encouraged that the sincere effort you are making is helping to develop a new neuropathway in your brain and nervous system.

If you are still very restless and feel you *must* move, you can do so slowly and consciously. Then resume your meditation. Or you can get up and do a walking meditation. Instructions for walking meditation are in chapter 4.

CHAPTER 4

MEDITATION VARIATIONS

Once you have attained even the smallest skill at the mechanics of meditation, you can apply it to more than simple breath meditation. Keep in mind that meditation is a state where you gain some steadiness of mind so there is not so much mind wandering. Once you have that steadiness, you can use your alertness to examine a myriad of different things.

Following are a few examples of variations on meditation practice:

- Mindful Meditation
- Walking Meditation
- Body Scan
- Heart Coherence
- Loving Kindness
- Contemplation
- Self- inquiry

At this point, we will now look at how to practice these other forms of meditation.

Mindfulness

Mindfulness is getting a lot of attention these days and seems to be the new hip thing. But what is it?

Mindfulness is essentially paying attention in the present moment to what is happening, around and inside of us, with an open and nonjudgmental awareness. It is a 'present moment awareness' with an attitude of acceptance and allowing. It is a nonjudgmental state of bare awareness.

Mindful Awareness in Meditation

Essentially, we apply mindfulness—or present moment awareness—to all of our meditation practice, no matter what kind of meditation we are doing.

Meditation is, inherently, being mindful. In meditation you are practicing being in the present moment, not thinking of past or future.

The three main places to practice being mindful are noticing:

- Thoughts
- Feelings
- Sensations

Mindful meditation is begun by first building your concentration by practicing staying focused on your breath. Once this brain muscle of concentration is sufficiently trained, then you can more easily apply mindful awareness to thoughts, feelings and sensations as they arise in meditation. But first practice breath meditation for a number of sessions.

Mindful Exploration

When something strong comes up and grabs your attention while meditating (or any other time) and you can't let it go, a useful way to be mindful or present with it is to ask these questions:

a. What is it?
b. How strong is it?
c. How long does it last?

Be open and curious as you ask these questions and observe. Simultaneously, stay focused on your breath. Your breath will keep you steady as you watch without judgment.

Don't get into mental chatter or analysis. This is very important. In applying these questions, you can observe your experience without getting caught in it. In this way you can be with your experience and accompany it while being with the breath. You are not figuring it out. You are not pushing it away. You are allowing it, without judgment, watching the experience and experiencing it, just as it is.

Walking Meditation

This can also be called conscious walking. With walking meditation we focus on the sensation of walking rather than the breath.

Begin in a standing posture. Feel yourself standing where you are. Notice the contact of your feet on the ground, or notice the sole of your foot connected to the sole of your shoe. Feel the quality of that contact and that your whole body is balanced over your feet. Here you are, standing.

As you get ready to move, drop your gaze to about six feet ahead of you. As you walk, make a mental note of your movements as they happen. You don't have to note each tiny movement. Noting a few movements is fine. The point is to stay in the present moment with what is happening: walking.

As a starting point, focus on the contact between your foot and the ground and the sensation of movement as you lift, push and drop each foot.

As you get the hang of it, you can add other mental notes such as:

> Raising
>
> Touching
>
> Pressing
>
> Shifting
>
> Swaying

If you get lost in thought, stop and note where your mind has been—"thinking," "planning," "daydreaming,"—and come back to conscious walking.

Body Scan Meditation

Body scan meditation can be extremely relaxing, especially once you get the hang of it. Some people use it to help get to sleep.

Body scan is typically done lying down. If you can, pick a firm place on a carpeted floor or some other comfortable spot. I avoid meditating on my bed because I fall asleep easier there. If you are really tired, you can do the body scan sitting up.

Start by closing your eyes and feeling the weight of your body relaxing onto the floor. Take a few moments to feel your breath and your whole body laying down.

Then systematically scan through your body, part by part. It is typical to start at the feet, move to the calves, thighs, hips, pelvis, etc.

Bring your full attention to each part of the body, one by one. Notice what is there. What is the sensation? Feel into that body part. How does it feel? You are not imagining. You are noticing. Heavy? Light? Soft? Tense? Numb? Nothing at all? Whatever you notice, simply notice without judgment. It can be helpful to take an attitude of open curiosity as you explore the sensation in each body part.

Body scan is great to do as a guided meditation. There are many guided body scan meditations on the internet for your enjoyment and support.

Heart Coherence Meditation

This meditation helps us to shift from mental activity to a more heart-centered focus.

Begin with a comfortable sitting posture. You can have your eyes open or closed. Follow these three steps:

1. Heart Focus: Shift your attention to the center of your chest and notice your heart and the heart space around it. It can be helpful to imagine an elevator dropping from your head down to your heart area.

2. Heart Focused Breathing: Take some slow easy breaths in and out. Pretend like the breath is breathing in and out of your heart.

3. Heart Feeling: Activate a positive emotion by recalling a time you felt positive emotions, a time when you felt joyful, happy, grateful or appreciative. Or think of gratitude that you have for something in your life, or appreciation you have for someone in your life, or maybe some compassion you feel for someone. Feel this feeling as best you can while continuing to breathe through the heart.

If you get distracted, simply come back to your breath, the heart and the positive feeling.

When you're finished, see if you can stay with the positive feeling as long as you can as you proceed with your day.

Loving Kindness Meditation

Loving kindness meditation is a way to cultivate compassion in our heart, for ourselves, others, and the world. Compassion can help us bear the pain that shows up in our lives, whether it be personal, with the people around us, or in the state of the world. It helps us to soften our heart and be more open to life as it presents itself.

In loving kindness meditation, we use a phrase of loving kindness as our point of focus, rather than the breath. With our attention on the phrase, we repeat it slowly to ourselves or out loud.

You can begin by focusing on yourself. Say the phrase first for yourself, repeating it two or more times:

May I be safe, be happy, be healthy, live with ease.

Then you can extend it to others. This can be people you love, people you know are hurting, people who you see every now and again (like your store clerk or mail delivery person), and to people with whom you are having difficulty.

Select who you would like to offer loving kindness to. Bring them to mind and repeat the phrase two or more times:

> *May you be safe, be happy, be healthy, live with ease.*

You can do this with as many people as you like.

And then you can offer loving kindness to the whole world, the planet, and all beings:

> *May all beings be safe, be happy, be healthy, live with ease.*

Contemplative Meditation

This meditation uses the clear and alert state of mind during meditation to examine a phrase or subject. Contemplation is another form of concentration. It allows for a focused attention on one thing. The more concentration you have, the more penetrating your contemplation will be. Most commonly, it is associated with studying religious or spiritual texts. It is by no means limited to the sacred and spiritual.

In contemplation you take a phrase and think about its meaning. You can break up the phrase into parts, think about the whole phrase altogether, contemplate one word at a time, or whatever works for you. Like all meditation, if your mind wanders, simply come back to your point of focus.

Here is a Zen koan to contemplate:

> *"Quick! Before thinking, right or wrong, what is your original face before your parents were born?"*

Or here is a Christian scripture to contemplate:

> "Look, I have set before you an open door, which no one is able to shut." Revelations 3:8

Any religious or inspirational text can be used. The gift of contemplation is that as we contemplate, we permeate deeper and deeper layers of thought and consciousness.

Self Inquiry

You can also use self-inquiry as a meditation focus, using a phrase such as:

> "Who am I?"
>
> "What is this awareness within me that is aware?"
>
> "Who is experiencing this experience?"

Pick one question and go with it. Self inquiry has been used successfully by many spiritual practitioners to break out of their normal habitual way of seeing themselves and the world.

CHAPTER 5

WHY MEDITATE?

Meditation is the opportunity to get to know yourself in an intimate way. It can deepen your connection to yourself, to Spirit/God/Presence (whatever you name it) and to life in general.

And, meditation can improve:

- creative thinking
- energy
- stress levels
- cognitive function
- peace of mind
- even success

Meditation can:

- protect telomeres for healthy aging
- support cellular health

Meditation can reduce:

- stress
- anxiety
- addiction
- depression
- eating disorders
- blood pressure
- pain response
- stress hormone levels

What's Your Motivation?

Because meditation is challenging at the beginning, you have to have a reason to meditate that is stronger than "it's a good idea," or "I heard it was good for me."

Why do you want to meditate? What is your motivation? Do you have a motivation that is connected to a higher vision of what you want for you and your life?

Are you looking for ease to your suffering? Do you want to get closer to Spirit/God? Do you want to steady your mind so you can peer a little deeper into Reality, improve physical or mental health? Some people are motivated to meditate because they feel like it not only helps them, it helps the world. Many people want more peace. What is calling you to meditation?

Another way to look at it is, what are you committed to? I have a commitment to transforming consciousness and to being my best self. This commitment is inspiring enough that it helps me continue with my practice day after day, year after year. It also motivates me to retreat at least twice a year.

Are you committed to something that will bring you back to the cushion again and again? What is it?

Your motivation to meditate will keep you practicing day after day, year after year. And that is a big deal. That is where transformation happens.

How to Keep Your Practice Going

Besides having a good motivation, it is helpful to have other support in your life to keep your meditation practice going. Here are things we have found helpful—and shall we say even essential—to keeping a regular meditation practice and making progress:

1. Meditate regularly with a group (weekly if you can).

2. Find a good meditation teacher who can guide you in your practice.

3. Having a dedicated place in your home for your practice, be it a chair, or corner, a nook, or even a room, is very helpful. What you do in

that place is meditate. Period. (However, if it is not possible to have a dedicated place, meditate in the same spot every day, if you can.)

4. Take a yearly meditation retreat—two if you can. Retreat is where you make progress forward with your practice. It is also a very effective way to re-boot or re-energize your practice when it is feeling dull or if you feel like you have plateaued.

We hope this book has inspired you and is supportive to you in starting a meditation practice or keeping your current one going.

Happy meditating!

RECOMMENDED READING

Mindfulness in Plain English, by Bhante Gunaratana

Real Happiness: The Power of Meditation: a 28 Day Program, by Sharon Salzberg

Radical Acceptance, Embracing Your Life With the Heart of a Buddha, by Tara Brach

Why Can't I Meditate?, by Nigel Wellings

True Meditation, by Adyashanti

Autobiography of A Yogi, by Paramahamsa Yogananda

Although the books below are not beginner's books, they are rich and valuable.

How to Know God, The Yoga Aphorisms of Pantanjali, translated with a commentary by Swami Prabhavananda and Christopher Isherwood.

The Dhammapada, introduced and translated by Eknath Easwaran

For questions or guidance, Lauren can be reached at www.healingandtransformation.com.

Made in United States
North Haven, CT
28 January 2025

65094258R00024